T0380939

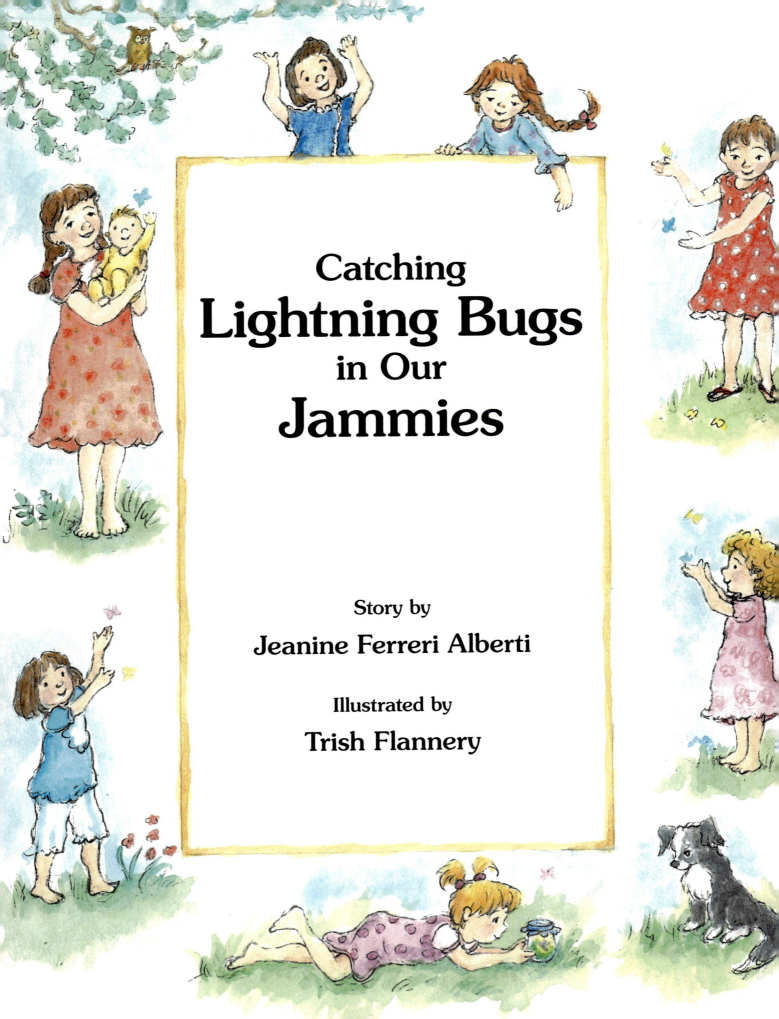

Catching
Lightning Bugs
in Our
Jammies

Story by

Jeanine Ferreri Alberti

Illustrated by

Trish Flannery

To order additional copies of this book, contact:
Xlibris
844-714-8691
www.Xlibris.com
Orders@Xlibris.com

ISBN: Softcover   979-8-3694-2639-5
               Hardcover   979-8-3694-2640-1
               EBook   979-8-3694-2638-8

Library of Congress Control Number: 2024915382

Print information available on the last page

Rev. date: 08/05/2024

Lightning Bugs by Fynnigan

It was the heart of Summer. The electric fans were buzzing loudly in the windows.

1

My grandparent's tomato vines were taller than Grandma! Barely five feet tall, my Italian grandma had the green thumb of a giant!

2

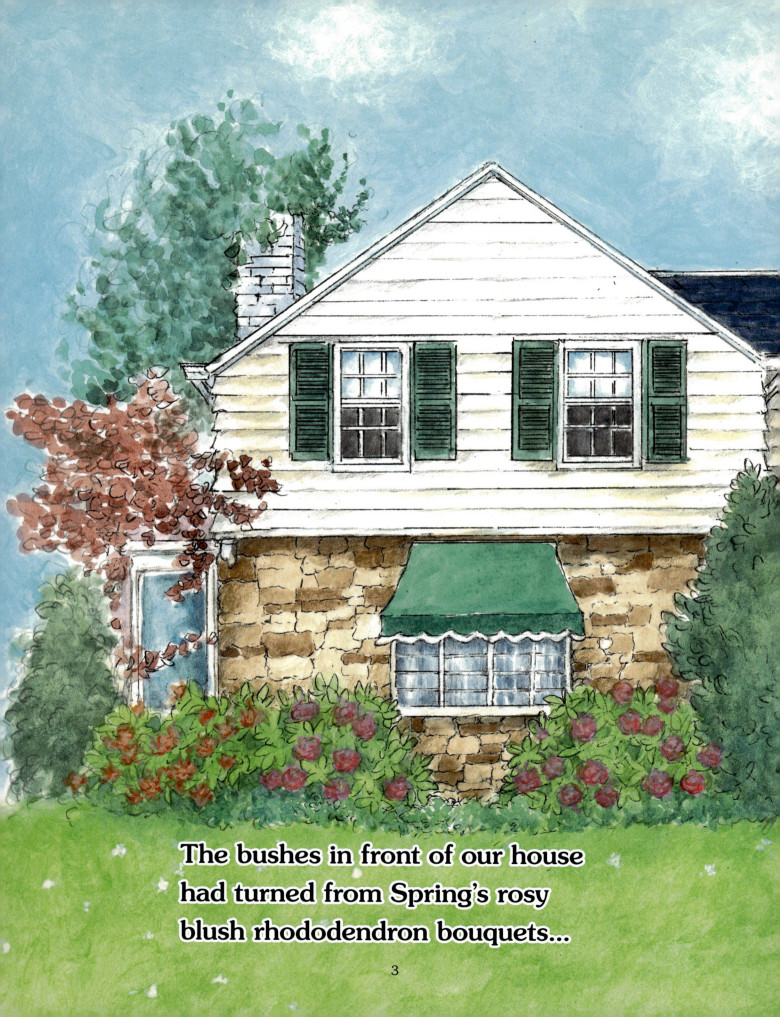

The bushes in front of our house
had turned from Spring's rosy
blush rhododendron bouquets...

...and sherbet orange azalea blossoms to Summer's deep verdant vivid green.

4

Lazy days were filled with enjoyment and laughter and an occasional difference of opinion. There were eight of us kids, after all!

The new bright yellow Slip 'N Slide was an intriguing addition to the sprinkler and small blow up pool that kept us cool.

On rainy days, we played Racko, one of our favorite card games, on the side porch.

7

We would
curl up there,
too, with our
library books
listening to the
gentle rain.

When the flowers were in bloom, we made "Peony Perfume" from their fragrant pink and white petals.

We squished them in beach buckets of water and then strained and bottled our glorious concoction. Yes, our days were quite carefree and full of delight and joy.

Almost every house on our street had kids. In the evening, folks filtered out of their homes to enjoy each others' company.

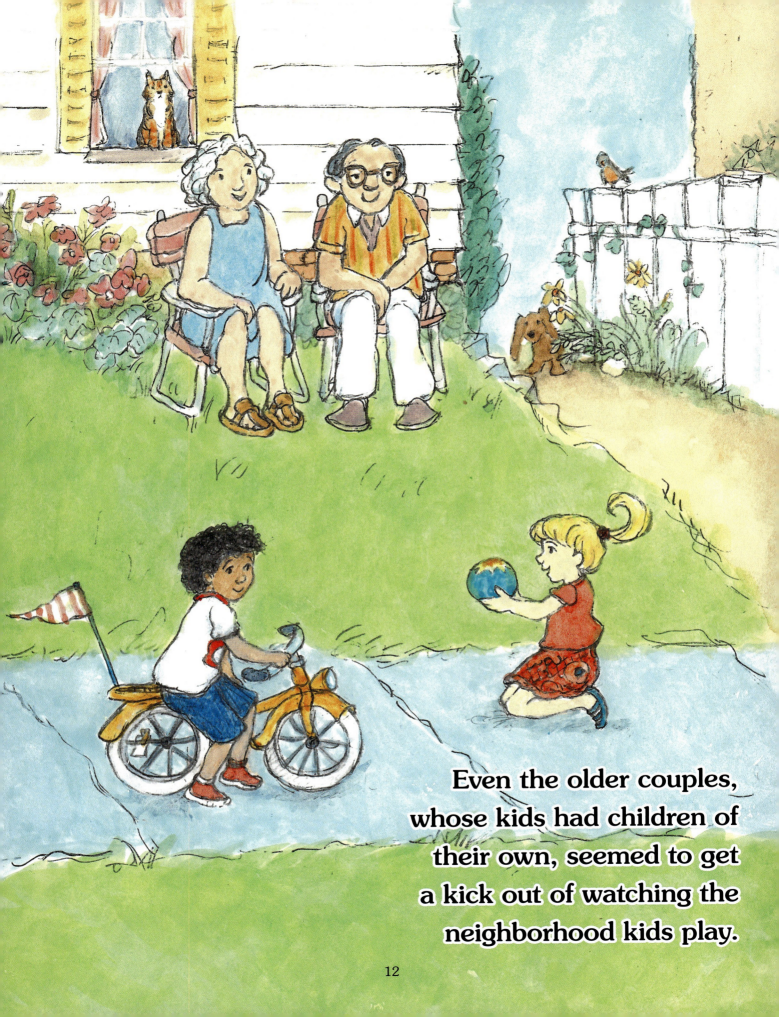

Even the older couples,
whose kids had children of
their own, seemed to get
a kick out of watching the
neighborhood kids play.

Dad counted for us as we had exciting Hula Hoop contests. Some of us were excellent Hula Hoopers!

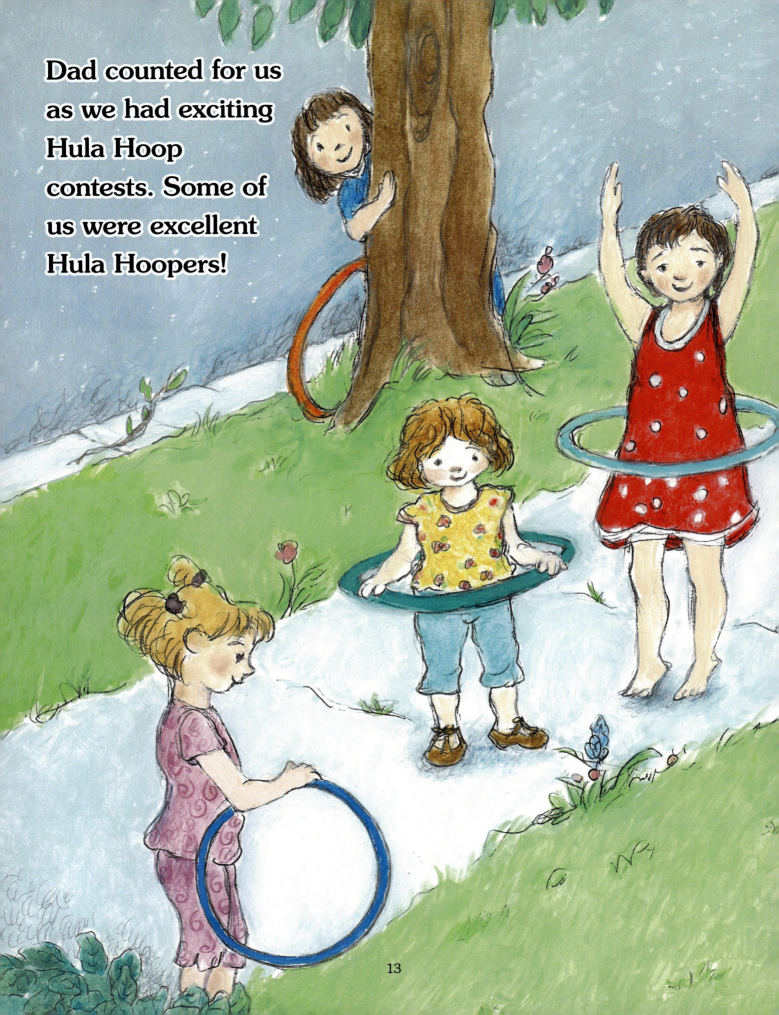

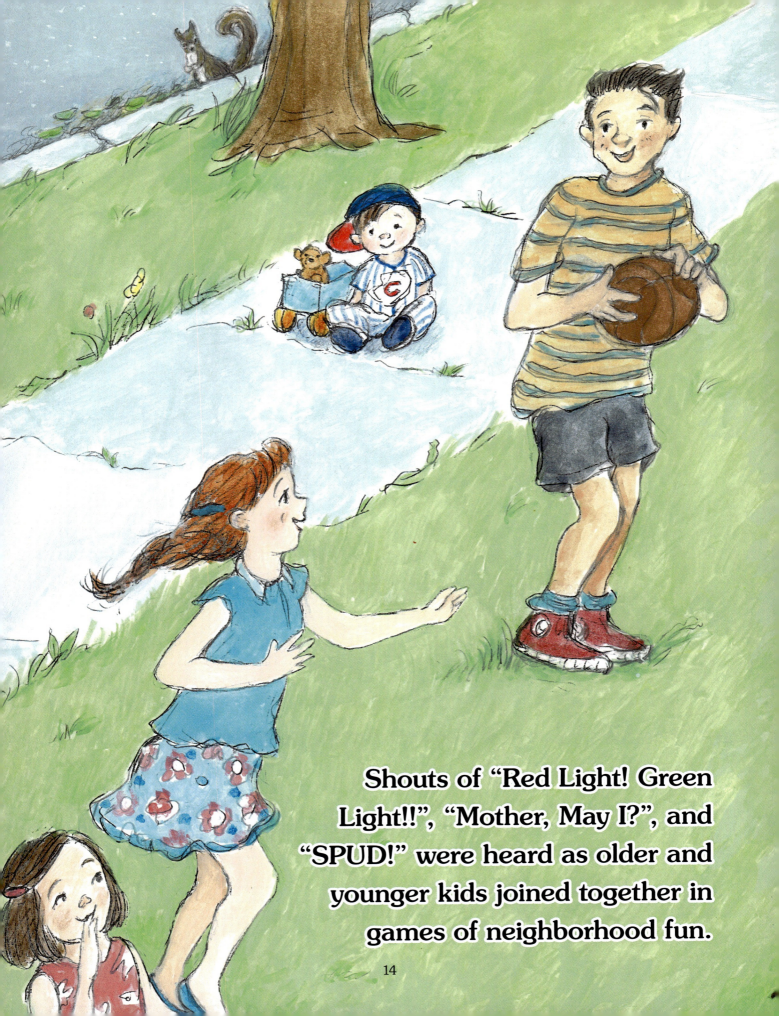

Shouts of "Red Light! Green Light!!", "Mother, May I?", and "SPUD!" were heard as older and younger kids joined together in games of neighborhood fun.

Sometimes, the older boys played
a kind of baseball in front of our
house. They usually called it "Five
Dollars" or "500" when using a bat
or "Flies and Grounders" if they
were just using gloves and mitts.

Did I mention there
were seven girls
and one baby boy
in our family?

"KICK THE CAN" was
my most favorite game
of all. I prided myself on
finding a good hiding
spot.

I silently waited, almost holding my breath, for that perfect moment to run in and KICK THE CAN, saving those kids who had been caught. We played outside until the streetlights came on.

As dusk crept into evening, lightning bugs graced our yards, rising from the lawns. Their dancing lights illuminated the dark.

With their
arrival, we all
knew it was
July in Ohio!

20

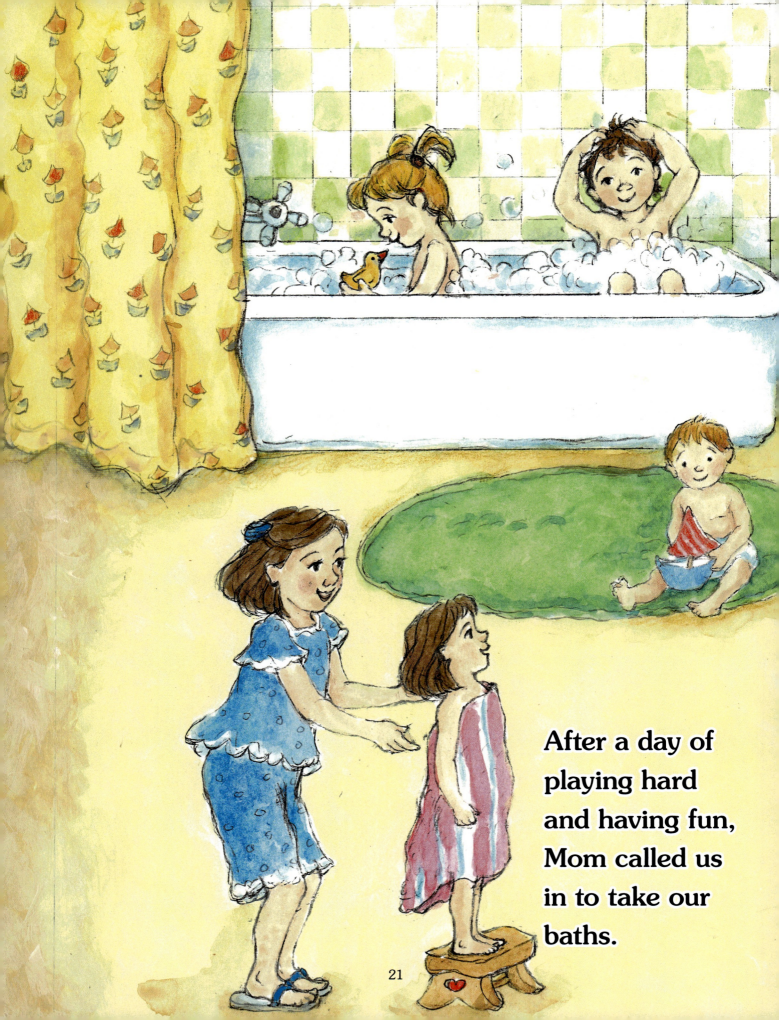

After a day of
playing hard
and having fun,
Mom called us
in to take our
baths.

21

It felt so good washing up and
putting on clean pajamas, or
"jammies" as we called them.

Then, we would be
allowed to go outside,
jammies and all,
before bedtime and
catch lightning bugs!

Funny, I wasn't a fan of bugs, but
I never even thought about having
a problem touching or catching a
lightning bug. After all, they were
magical... like little twinkling stars.

Sometimes, we would put the lightning bugs in a glass jar. A comfy bed of grass was added to the bottom.

To keep them safely inside, a piece of plastic wrap, secured with a rubber band, was placed on top. Carefully, holes were poked into it to allow in the cool evening air.

We were full of pure summertime joy, running around our yard with the night breeze blowing through our wet hair, catching those sparkly and enchanting lightning bugs.

27

Daddy and Mommy would watch us as they sat in their lawn chairs under the overhang of the garage.

Peace and contentment filled our hearts. Refreshing root beer floats, or "Black Cows" as Mom called them, filled our tummies. Wrapped in the love of family, all seemed right on those starry summer nights.

Lightning Bugs by Avery

How to play KICK THE CAN

Gather at least 6 or 7 friends together. Find an empty can… and begin a game that is like tag, hide-and-go-seek, and capture the flag all rolled into one! Decide on one friend to be "IT" and place the "CAN" in someone's driveway. The friend who is IT sits on or next to the CAN, with eyes closed, and counts to 30 (or any number decided by the group) while the rest of the kids run and hide. When the designated number has been reached, IT calls out, "Ready or not, here I come!" and starts to look for the hidden kids and tries to tag them, while also keeping an eye on the CAN. If IT tags a player, he or she goes " JAIL" , a place nearby the CAN and waits with others who have been tagged and caught. Any players still hiding, can run in and KICK THE CAN and set all the captured players free. If no players have been tagged and captured yet, then a hidden player can come running in, and just tap the CAN with a light touch so it DOESN'T fall over. He or she does NOT go to JAIL and remains free. The game ends when all the players have been caught or when the last hidden player runs in and KICKS THE CAN and frees everyone else.

by Fynnigan

How to play SPUD

SPUD is a blast to play, especially with at least 10 or more players! All you need is a big playground ball, and a bunch of friends. Have an adult or a friend who decides not to play, be THE NUMBER GIVER. If your group has 10 players, THE NUMBER GIVER whispers a number from 1-12 in each player's ear. If you have 12 players then the numbers given will be from 1-14. The extra two numbers are GHOST NUMBERS and no player will have them. DO NOT SHARE YOUR NUMBER! One player will be IT and will stand with the ball in the middle of a circle of players. IT throws the ball up into the air as he or she yells out a number. Everyone runs away unless it's your number that has been called. If so, catch or grab the ball as fast as you can, and yell out the word SPUD! Once SPUD has been yelled everyone running must stop! The player who caught the ball, then takes 3 giant steps towards any player and throws the ball at the player, who cannot move his or her feet. The thrower cannot throw at the player's head. If the ball hits the player, he or she gets the letter, "S". Now the player who got hit with the ball is IT and calls out a number as he or she throws the ball into the air. If it happens to be a GHOST NUMBER that no player has, all must FREEZE! Anyone who moves, including the thrower, gets a letter in the word SPUD. If you are a player who gets all the letters, S-P-U-D, you are out!

Lightning Bugs by Gianna

Look up some more fun games you can play with your friends. Ask your parents and grandparents for some suggestions, too. They may even play them with you!

Lilac by Fynnigan

Printed in the United States
by Baker & Taylor Publisher Services